Hello King

Written by Tacardra B. Rountree

Dedications

I dedicate this book to all the Kings that have impacted my life. I would like to especially recognize:
My Grandfathers, Charlie Rountree Jr. and Sammie Lee Dexter, the Kings that prayed for me;
My Father, Harold Rountree, the King that raised me;
My Uncle, Rev. James Scruggs, the King that spiritually guides me;
and S.R., the King that loves me.

I honor Kings of the past, recognize Kings of the present, and rejoice about the Kings of the future.

Thank you to the King of Kings and Lord of Lords. May all that I do glorify you.

This book belongs to

King

____

I am an African King.

I am filled with hopes and dreams.

My present is bright and my future is promising.

Truth and knowledge is what I seek.

I am intelligent.

I walk with confidence.

I stand proudly on the shoulders of my ancestors.

I am a light for the world to see.

I am courageous when challenges come my way.

There is a leader in me.

I will make wise choices.

I have the power to make positive changes.

I will think before I speak.

I will uplift others.

I will support and respect the Queen.

I can be whatever I choose to be.

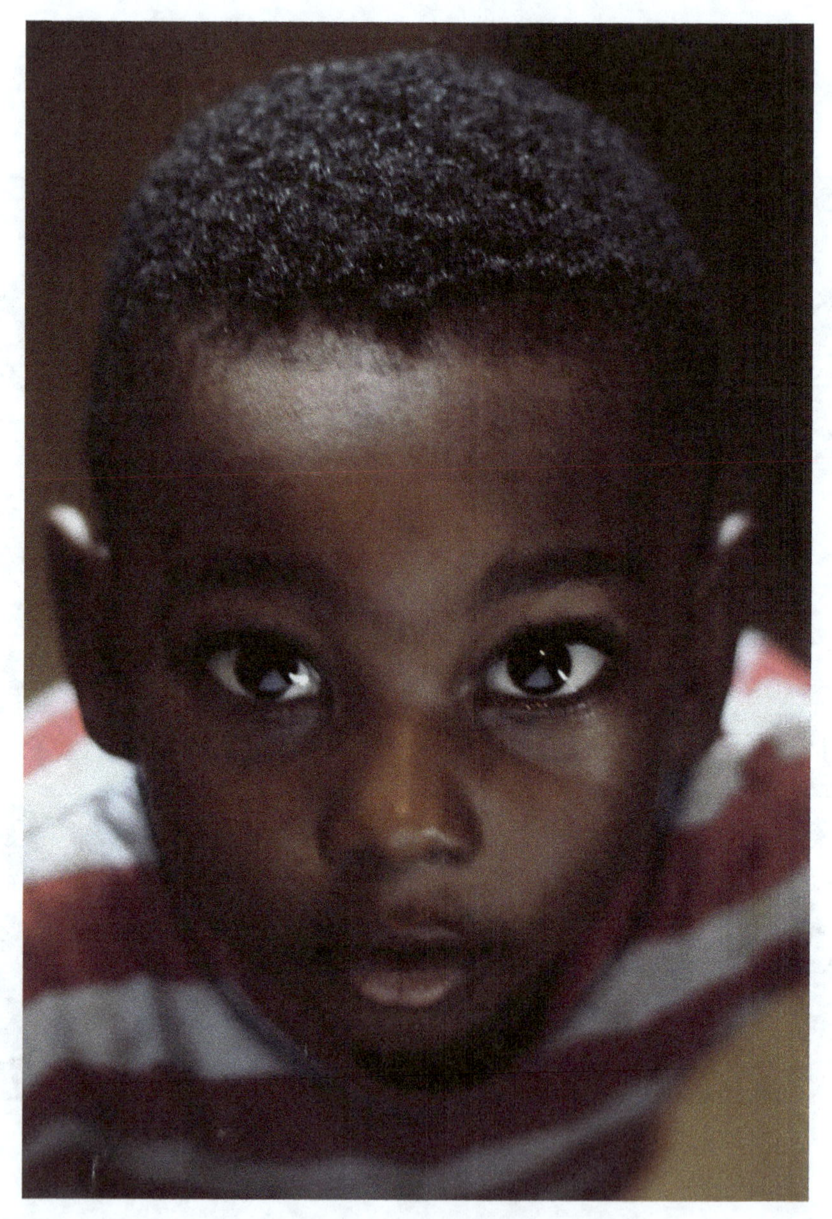

I will not give up.

I will keep going.

I am a success.

My life has a purpose.

My life has meaning.

I will continue my journey because I know who I am.

Who am I?

wise
successful
thinker
confident
intelligent
supporter
leader
I Am An African King!

Hello King
Written By Tacardra B. Rountree

I am an African King.
I am filled with hopes and dreams.
My present is bright and my future is promising.
Truth and knowledge is what I seek.
I am intelligent.
I walk with confidence.
I stand proudly on the shoulders of my ancestors.
I am a light for the world to see.
I am courageous when challenges come my way.
There is a leader in me.
I will make wise choices.
I have the power to make positive changes.
I will think before I speak.
I will uplift others.
I will support and respect the Queen.
I can be whatever I choose to be.
I will not give up.
I will keep going.
I am a success.
My life has a purpose.
My life has meaning.
I will continue my journey because I know who I am.
Who am I?
I am an African King.

For author visits, speaking engagements, and conference presentations, please connect through the following:

Website: https://authortrountree.com
Facebook: T.B. Rountree
Instagram: @authortrountree